# CONTENTS

D0177645

Published by Grandreams, Jadwin House,
205/211 Kentish Town Road, London NW5
Printed in Holland. 0 86227 043 X.

Pet's Corner features written by Beryl Johnston. © 1981 Grandreams.
Remaining features © Barbara Woodhouse.
Picture of Juno (page 53) © Michael Woodhouse.
Main pic front cover, page 17 and main pic 26-27 © Grandreams taken by
Nigel I. Money. Remaining pictures supplied by Bruce Coleman Limited.
Edited by John Barraclough, Layout and design, Nigel I. Money.

£2.25

# Hello from
# BARBARA WOODHOUSE

I believe that keeping animals should be fun.
Therefore this book will show a lot of animals that
you can keep whether it is a pony or a tiny hamster.
If you can't have a pony help other people with
theirs.
If you have a dog train it to be obedient and go in
for the amateur obedience competitions often put on
at exceptional dog shows.
If you are very busy, birds like canaries or
budgerigars don't take up much time, but give you a
lot of pleasure.
Animals and birds are a great responsibility, see
that you look after them personally and never think
they can take care of themselves. Lots of children,
starting in a small way, have ended up by being the
tops in the show world with their pets.
My motto with animals is: 'Be fair, be firm and be
fun'.
Yours ever

*Barbara Woodhouse*

*Below:* German Shepherd Dog.

# Choosing Your Dog

IN a book of this kind it is impossible to examine in detail all the breeds of dogs, their advantages and disadvantages. I can, however, give you a little general guidance In your choice.

Dogs fall roughly into three groups: sporting breeds, non-sporting breeds and toy dogs. In the first come the terriers, which seem to appeal to people living in the country with facilities for plenty of exercise and freedom. The most popular are the Airedale, Australian Terrier, Bedlington, Border Terrier, Bull Terrier, Cairn Terrier, Dandie Dinmont Terrier, Fox Terrier, Irish Terrier, Kerry Blue, Lakeland Terrier, Manchester Terrier, Norwich Terrier, Sealyham, Skye Terrier, Staffordshire Bull Terrier, and West Highland White Terrier.

I would not advise buying a terrier unless you have time to exercise and train it, for by nature it is a working dog. Without proper occupation it is inclined to get bored and irritable. This sometimes leads to it be pugnacious and unfriendly with other dogs. Always remember that it is more inclined to bark than a less active dog.

In the non-sporting class come the Boston Terrier, Bearded Collie, Boxer, Bulldog, Bullmastiff, Chow-chow, Collie, Dalmatian, French Bulldog, Great Dane, Keeshond, Mastiff, Newfoundland, Old English Sheepdog, Poodle, St Bernard, Samoyed, Schipperke, Schnauzer, Shetland Sheepdog, Shi Tzu and Welsh Corgi.

Also in this group, in spite of the misleading name, are some dogs with a job of work to do. For example, one of the best known and most popular dogs in this country is the Alsatian, now called a German Shepherd Dog. None is better fitted to carry out strenuous work, which accounts for its frequent selection as a guard dog. If properly trained it is a gentle and faithful friend to all members of the family, often allowing the small baby to climb over it and pull its ears. On the other hand, there has grown into some strains an extreme nervousness which makes them unsafe in some cases. So, when choosing a dog—and this applies to any breed—visit the parents of the puppy, and don't buy if either parent has a nervous or vicious temperament and beware of a deformity, i.e. hip dysplasia.

Then there are the toy dogs, heart stealers all. The Pekinese, the English Toy Terrier, the Griffon—a monkey like dog of great intelligence—the Pomeranian, which as a puppy fits into a tea cup and, full grown, sometimes into a large breakfast cup, the Pug so well beloved of our ancestors, and the Yorkshire Terrier who will tackle a rat nearly twice its own size.

Only you can decide whether you want a big dog, a medium-sized dog or a small one. The type you keep depends largely on the amount of time and money you have. Big dogs can cost up to £6 a week to keep, and a dog that needs constant trimming to keep it healthy and beautiful can be a strain on both owner and his pocket. The main thing to remember is that the dog you fancy is probably the dog you will be happiest with. If you are persuaded to choose something you don't want, you will blame the breed if it later shows any unpleasant characteristics.

If I wanted a large dog I should choose a Great Dane or a Bullmastiff or, among the sporting dogs, English Setter or a Flat-coat Retriever, for on the whole they have placid, reliable temperaments, are good with children and learn to obey easily.

Many people cannot resist a Spaniel of which there are many varieties, among them the Cockers, American Cockers, Clumbers, Springers, Field Spaniels, etc. But again Spaniels need work to be really

5

Basset-Hound puppies

happy, and some modern Cockers especially the Golden are a bit unreliable in temperament and bite their owners. I think that any breed that has had extensive popularity gets bred in large numbers to the final detriment of temperament. To make money the owners of the bitches breed without regard to any nervous temperament the puppies may show once they are sold.

Poodles too are enormously popular and enjoying an ever-increasing vogue, while the Dachshund (long- or short-coated variety) makes a delightful pet when obedience trained—seldom showing bad temperament and easily looked after.

If you want a sporting little dog that eats very little and is always ready for a game, an English Toy Terrier or Miniature Pinscher Terrier, is hard to beat. On the other hand, if you are a bit on the lazy side, a King Charles Spaniel will stay happily in the house or garden with you. If you are likely to be abroad a lot, don't buy a Great Dane. They break their hearts when left. If you want to show your friends what a good dog trainer you are, buy an Alsatian, a Dobermann Pinscher, a Shetland Sheepdog or the fashionable Poodle. All these are easily and quickly trained. If you want to be stared at and envied by all you meet, have a Pyrenean Mountain dog, or a Maremma Sheepdog. These beautiful creatures get admiration wherever they go. For an all-round little sport a Cairn or a West Highland fills the bill. Border Collies, attractive and easily trained, make delightful pets too, but training is essential to get the best out of them. They must have work or they sometimes get neurotic.

If the dog is to live outside and be a guard, he must be a hardy type of dog; but if he is to be a house dog this is not so important.

Mongrels are, of course, by far the most popular dog in this country. However, when I am asked whether I would advise buying a mongrel or a pure bred, I always advise the pure bred. It costs no more to feed, and you do know from the start how big a dog you are buying. Pride of ownership counts for a lot too.

To sum up, if you have plenty of time to exercise and groom the dog, and your house is big, just buy any dog you fancy, for it is your training that will make or mar whatever you choose. But no matter what the result, you should never blame the faults on the breed.

All dogs need the same things: a good home, good food, a firm but understanding owner, plenty of praise and love, and a peaceful end when their days are nearly over.

7

# Feeding, Grooming, Exercising

IT is not an easy task to lay down the law on how to feed your dog. Like human beings, all dogs have their own likes and dislikes, and what might suit the dog next door, and keep it in perfect health, might make your dog a miserable specimen. But as a rule, simplicity in diet is the thing to aim for.

All dogs, being carnivorous creatures, should have meat in some form daily, although it is not unknown for some to be perfectly healthy on a vegetarian diet.

There are vast numbers of patent dog foods now on the market, and if you have any doubts about what to give your dog, you can safely rely on well known brands to keep him in perfect health. Many households with only one dog find that they have ample scraps left over for him. If all the food is soft, however, the dog's teeth and gums will suffer. To prevent this he should be given a large bone to eat occasionally. That will do a lot towards keeping healthy gums. Unhealthy gums often cause bad breath.

A puppy at weaning time, say at six weeks, should have four to five meals a day, two consisting of brown bread and milk, or some proprietary brand of food, and two of minced raw beef. To encourage the puppy to chew its food it is a good idea to give biscuit for one meal, hard and dry.

As the puppy grows older the number of meals is slowly reduced, until at six months and over he is having two meals a day, the largest at night, so that he sleeps quietly until morning. The amounts given depend on the condition and the exercise taken by the dog. Some people complain that their dogs seem to require only one meal a day. Well, if that is the case you needn't worry. Give one meal a day, a mixture of his meat ration in some form, and his brown bread or biscuit ration, all at the same time.

It is commonly heard that dogs need vegetables to keep them healthy. This is, I am sure, a fallacy. Some dogs like vegetables, and a little of what you fancy undoubtedly does you good. But dogs were not made to eat vegetables, and the eating of grass in no way indicates that they need them. When a dog eats grass its digestion is out of order and it hopes by so doing to make itself sick. But I have known dogs who loved eating raspberries and blackberries off the bushes. I have known others to eat apples in a gluttonous way. My own Juno adored strawberry juice, and when we had a tin of strawberries she always had the liquid. But these are fads and fancies rather than the diet of a normal dog.

What a dog does need are vitamins, and unless they exist in good supply in his normal diet, it is quite essential to add vitamins A and B to his food. These are nowadays bought in pills from the chemist and present no difficulty to the dog owner, and an additive like Vionate supplies the trace elements of minerals dogs often lack in their diet.

It is very wrong to feed your dog between meals. This will make him fat and unhealthy, and nothing is more revolting that an overfed dog as a companion. In my opinion, it is wrong too to let him watch expectantly while you are eating your own meal. For when he is expecting food his saliva runs, and if not given something to eat his digestion may get upset. The dog should always be ready at a set time to have his meal. In fact dogs make very good clocks. Mine always knew their meal times to the second, and I was reminded by them both as they lay with their heads on their paws, watching me with imploring eyes, that I was wanted at once to get their dinner.

## GROOMING

I feel sure that most dog owners will be willing to give up five minutes a day to grooming. It improves looks and health of both long- and short-coated dogs. And not only that, the friction improves the health of the skin. But be sure you use the right grooming implements. A wire comb is not suitable for a dog with a short coat, like a Corgi, who is best groomed with a glove brush. A Poodle, on the other hand, needs both a wire brush and wire comb to get through the mat of hair. One of the most difficult dogs to keep tidy is a Cocker Spaniel, for his ears are so easily matted, and it is not unknown for them to have become so tangled through lack of proper attention that the dog has had to go to a vet and have an anaesthetic before the tangles could be combed out or cut. So if you own one of this breed, do be sure to brush and comb it daily, especially after a walk in the mud.

After a muddy walk, many dogs clean

*Two delightful Cocker Spaniels. Although very popular with children they are, however, difficult dogs to keep tidy and need daily combing and brushing.*

*Longhaired and Shorthaired Dachshunds*

themselves in a remarkable way if given clean straw to dry off in. Collies are well known to look spotless in no time at all. But it is always advisable to dry any dog that has got wet.

Groom your dog firmly and kindly and he will enjoy it. It is a disgrace to have a dog contaminated with insects. If there is a chance of this, use a good dog insect powder. Always examine the coat by blowing back the hair to make certain there is no infestation. Bathing is not good for all dogs' coats, as it softens them, but unless you have a show dog, a bath is the best way of keeping the coat clean and healthy. I think once a month is often enough. Always use a good dog soap, as it is a protection against skin troubles and insects. Be sure not to let the water get into the dog's ears or eyes, and never let his head go under water or you may frighten him. Let him have a good shake and then rub him down, and keep him indoors until he is dry.

## EXERCISE

A lot of nonsense is talked about the amount of exercise a dog needs, and many owners go out in very inclement weather in the mistaken idea that their pet will fall ill if not taken for long walks twice a day. A naturally happy, affectionate dog, if allowed the freedom of the house, follows members of the family about quite a lot of the day, and thereby gets a fair amount of exercise. All dogs love a long exciting walk, but it cannot do them much good to be taken out in wet and sometimes freezing weather, simply to fulfil what their owners imagine to be their duty towards them. My dogs always got two runs a day and went everywhere I went, but if the weather was bad they got the minimum of exercise necessary for cleanliness and health, and everyone remarked on their beautiful condition. Dogs do, however, look forward to a really long walk in the country on weekends, and know only too well the day of the week.

As a general rule half an hour a day is adequate exercise for most dogs, plus the bits and pieces they get when they accompany their owner shopping.

A good romp with a ball or a neighbour's dog goes a long way to keeping your pet fit. But never throw stones for him. They are easily swallowed and can damage the mouth. Hide your handkerchief and make your dog find it, or make him sit while you run away and hide. That makes the exercise fun and will do him much more good than miles on a lead. Never let him off the lead in the street. Find a quiet field or park away from traffic before even the best behaved dog is allowed to run free.

# DOG CROSSWORD

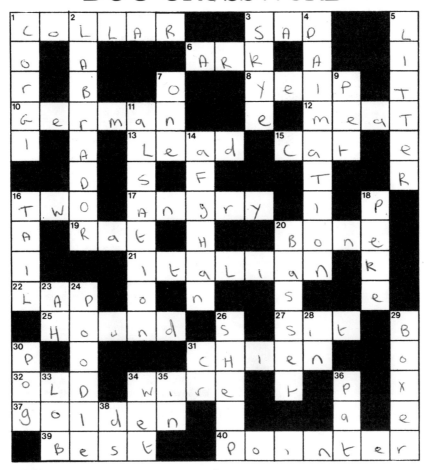

The completed grid shows the following filled answers:

1 across: COLLAR / 3: SAD / L
COR / 6: ARK / A / I
AR / O / 8: YELP / P / T
10: GERMAN / 12: MEAT / T
I / 13: LEAD / 15: CAT / E
DS / F / TI / R
16: TWO / 17: ANGRY / TI / 18: P
A / 19: RAT / H / 20: BONE
I / 21: ITALIAN / K
22: LAP / O / N / S / E
25: HOUND / 26: S / 27: SIT / 29: B
30: P / O / 31: CHIEN / O
32: OLD / 34: WIRE / H / 36: P / X
37: GOLDEN / 38: DEN / A / E
39: BEST / 40: POINTER

## ACROSS

1 Keep this around your dog's neck and it should never go astray.
3 A bloodhound happy? Never! — It always looks the opposite.
6 Noah kept his dogs here, together with his other animals.
8 Your dog will make this noise if it is hurt.
10 A _____ Shepherd Dog is another name for an Alsatian.
12 Give your dog lots of this to keep it fit
13 This usually accompanies 1 across.
15 Normally a dog will give chase when seeing one of these.
16 When a young puppy is given _____ injections to prevent disease.
17 If you pull a dog's tail it will only get _____.
19 In olden times Jack Russell Terriers were trained to catch this pest.
20 Give this to your dog and it will soon bury it.
21 This small breed of Greyhound I'm sure doesn't eat spaghetti, or does it?
22 Let small dogs sit on your _____ but with big dogs beware!
25 Huckleberry _____ is a well-known cartoon character.
27 Mrs Woodhouse is famous for saying this command.
31 The french word for 'Dog'.
32 The _____ English Sheepdog is also known as a Bobtail.
34 The _____-haired fox terrier does have fur, believe it or not.
37 A retriever can be black or _____.
39 At Crufts to become best in a show a dog must firstly become _____ of breed.
40 This breed of dog is not rude when it does as it's name implies.

## DOWN

1 These dogs are often seen at Buckingham Palace.
2 These dogs make very good guide dogs for the blind.
3 You do not have to look up at the clouds to see this breed of terrier.
4 You can't knock the spots off this dog!
5 A _____ is the name given to a group of puppies.
7 One hundred and _____ dalmations.
9 A dog at home is the family _____.
11 You often see this dog with a policeman.
14 This breed of dog originates from Afghanistan.
16 A dog will wag this when it is happy.
18 The short name for a Pekinese.
20 This hound has short dumpy legs, a long body, sad eyes and long ears.
23 Make this noise to comfort your dog.
24 Miniature, Standard and Toy are all types of this dog.
26 Many breeds of dog are used by farmers to round up _____.
28 Most dogs like to walk and run outdoors rather than ____.
29 Never pick a fight with this dog!
30 K-9 is Doctor Who's _____.
31 ____ufts is the most famous dog show in the world.
33 _____ a ball in the air for your dog to catch.
34 A dog should always have a _____ nose.
35 D____go is an Australian breed of dog.
36 When your dog has been good _____ him on the head.
38 Walt __i__ney created the cartoon character 'Goofy'.

# Pet's Corner

## Rabbits

Rabbits make excellent pets and are very easy to keep. If you have a plot of grass that could be given over to your rabbits that is the best way to keep them. Move them at least once a day to get fresh grass and supplement this with odd scraps of vegetables, bread and milk or porridge and milk, oats and bran and in winter of course hay.

When making the hutch you have to construct two compartments; a day compartment consisting of a wood and wire run which fixes onto the box that you prepare as the bedroom. This must be three quarters shut in order to provide shelter against wind and weather and it makes a nice place for the doe to have her babies. Always put plenty of clean dry hay in the bedroom place. On top of the bedroom box should put a cover of felt or a sheet of tin raised one end higher than another to allow air to pass around or it might get damp. The run should have a large piece of corrugated iron to cover it up in bad or very windy weather, rabbits don't like rain. The bedroom must be kept scrupulously clean and it is best to put shavings or saw- dust under the hay to absorb the urine, then you can take the wet part out when you clean the cage out. Don't return the hutch to a very soiled part of grass or the rabbit will get ill. If the rabbit tries to escape from the hutch by burrowing you must put a very wide mesh wire-netting all across the floor so it can't burrow yet it can eat the grass underneath.

If you haven't got a grass patch you build your hutch on legs, creasoting the outer woodwork for weatherproo- fing. Always have the frame- work of the hutch outside or the rabbit may eat the wood, they like gnawing. Therefore leave carrots or root vegetables like swede to keep them amused, even an old piece of branch gives them the opportunity to gnaw and keep their teeth down. Rabbits' nails are inclined to grow very long unless they are kept on concrete so you want to keep an eye on this and if they begin to turn over get the Vet to cut them if you can't do it yourself with a guillotine nail cutter. Be very careful not to cut the quick. With white rabbits it is easy to see the quick but with black or brown ones it's not so easy.

If you want to breed you must make two cages and keep the buck away from the doe only letting her in with him for mating. Rabbits can be mated practically anytime, but always add the buck to the doe not the doe to the buck or they may fight. She carries her litter for anything between 28 and 32 or more days and the babies are born naked and blind, but by ten days old their eyes are open and the fur has grown. They mature amazingly fast and will soon begin nibbling their mothers food. Give the mother plenty of food not only when carrying the babies but afterwards to be sure that she has plenty of milk to feed them. They should be taken away from her at about 6 weeks old.

I don't believe a doe should be bred with before 6 months. Let them get fully mature, and don't breed unless you have the hope of being able to sell the babies either privately or to a pet shop.

To sex them catch the rabbit by the scruff of the neck and balance it's quarters on your other hand, you will then be able to see it's sex organs. The buck has a round shaped genital opening, the female a V shaped one. And of course the female has six teats for feeding her

*Left:* Domestic rabbit: fawn baby with agouti mother. *Above:* White Angora Rabbit Doe.

babies. I don't recommend that a doe has more than two litters a year if you intend keeping her some years. Let her get into really good condition before mating her. Increase the milk feed whilst she is 'in kindle'.

It all depends on what you want the rabbits for as to what breed you want. Very gentle ones are Dutch and Angora. With Angora you can collect the hair and get it eventually made into a garment for yourself. They have to be kept brushed to keep the fur clean and unmatted.

Watch for colds, running eyes and sneezing are the signals, take professional advice as pneumonia is a killer in rabbits.

If the rabbit keeps scratching or shaking its head it may have mites, ear mange or canker and again it will have to have a powder from

the pet shop or if bad from your Vet.

If you wish to breed rabbits commercially for meat you may wish to breed with Belgian hares, these are much larger than ordinary rabbits and put on flesh rapidly. Your butcher would probably buy all you could breed.

The Rex rabbit is a rabbit without overlength hairs which produces a lovely velveteen like appearance. I think I was the first person to produce this coat when I was at the Institute of Rabbit Husbandry. I inadvertantly left a cage open and an Angora escaped and mated with a wild rabbit and the offspring were all Rex rabbits.

When I was young we kept Beverans, Belgian hares and Dutch rabbits all very different in temperament and all very charming.

Ostrich

A

B

cat

Cow

C

Can you put a name to
each shape shown?

D

Camel

E

Giraffe

frog

Seal

G

F

Bat

H

I

Kangaroo

Shadow

hapes Quiz

J Horse

K Squirrel

M ~~Read~~ Polar Bear

L mouse

N crab

O Rhinoceros

P Penguin

Q snake

R crocodile

Answers on page 63.

# ANIMAL CROSSWORD

## ACROSS

- 1 A Butterfly starts out life as this. (11)
- 7 See 31 Down.
- 8 Don't copy this monkey (3)
- 10 The book 'A Ring of Bright Water' was based on this animal (5)
- 12 These insects live in large hills made of soil (7)
- 14 This animal's name sounds like a dessert (5)
- 17 This animal doesn't stop laughing (5)
- 18 The noise made by a sheep (5)
- 20 A female Rabbit (3)
- 21 A male Swan (3)
- 24 The Tortoise or the Hare? Well of course the Tortoise was this (6)
- 25 An alligator is often mistaken for this when floating in the river (3)
- 27 The name for a young male horse (4)
- 28 A young Eagle (5)
- 30 As strong as an ____. (2)
- 31 This sea creature is the largest mammal in the World (5)
- 33 What a Cheetah has in common with a Dalmation. (5)
- 34 You often see this through a Bull's nose (4)
- 36 The name for any animal kept at home (3)
- 38 Where an Ostrich buries its head (4)
- 39 Pop goes the _____ ! (6)
- 40 The partner of 5 Down (3)

## DOWN

- 1 Don't get near the jaws of this snappy creature. Or else! (9)
- 2 Blue, Great and Long-tailed are all types of which bird (3)
- 3 A Skunk will give off a strong smell when meeting this (5)
- 4 The White Rabbit from 'Alice in Wonderland' was always _____ (4)
- 5 A male Sheep. (3)
- 6 You will need one of these if you want to catch Butterflies (3)
- 9 Trafalgar Square is the home of this bird (6)
- 11 A type of Deer found in England (3)
- 13 You will often find this animal at home in his warren (6)
- 15 How many Partridges were sent on the first day of Christmas (3)
- 16 ____nta leaves his reindeer on the roof before coming down the chimney with presents (2)
- 17 In danger this animal will roll up into a tight ball (8)
- 19 The Tortoise of the sea (6)
- 22 A wise old bird (3)
- 23 This sea creature has eight arms. Or are they legs? (7)
- 26 A Fox's tail (5)
- 29 This black and white bird is always collecting things bright and shiny (6)
- 31, 37 & 7 Across. The _____ ____ _____ Willows by Kenneth Graeme (4,2,3)
- 32 Rhode Island Red is a type of C__icke__ (2)
- 33 The _____ Goose by Paul Gallico (4)
- 34 The smallest and weakest puppy in a litter (4)
- 37 See 31 Down.

# Training Dogs for Show

*Not everyone can have the pleasure of exhibiting their dogs at such a grand show as Crufts, but up and down the country there are many local shows in which you can enter your dog and I'm sure that at sometime during the year there must be one near you. Whatever standard the show, it is important that your dog is 'prepared' properly and on these pages and overleaf I demonstrate some show stances with the help of Dodie of Ascotheath, a dalmation bitch.* **Left:** *Walking to heel.* **Above:** *Show stance.*

# Crufts

I think everybody interested in dogs must have heard of Crufts show, it is the biggest show in the world, although Westminster show in New York runs very close to it.

Between 7,000 and 10,000 dogs go to this show every year, some breeds on the first day and the rest of the breeds the second day, so if you are interested in seeing a certain breed be sure to find out which day that breed is being shown.

You can't just enter a dog for Crufts, it has to qualify by winning a first in a certain class at a Championship Show, if you want to know all about this the Kennel Club, 1, Clarges Street London W.1. will always send you particulars of the rules.

The dogs are all shown in their breed classes, and the winners then enter the big ring at the end of each day to compete against each other for supreme champion at the end of the second day which is always televised by the B.B.C. The supreme champion becomes an exceedingly valuable dog and the puppies that he or she may sire or have could be sold all over the world.

People attend Crufts from all over the world and there is a special room put aside for them with interpretors so that if they want to buy a dog the sale can be put through there and then.

When you go to Crufts you will find much more than dogs there, you will find lots of stalls selling everything to do with the doggy kingdom from great ranges of kennels to trinkets in the shape of the different breeds. The dogs start arriving from as far away as Northern and Southern Ireland, Scotland and Wales, some of them have travelled with their owners overnight in special buses. No sooner have they arrived than the owners start grooming them; powdering the breeds that need it like Fox-Terriers, Old English Sheepdogs etc; The small dogs are placed on tables to do this. The tables are brought by the owners, in fact a tremendous amount of beautifying equipment is brought by the owners to the show. The Afghans take a lot of grooming, the owners all know that the judge expects a dog to be presented in perfect condition and the coat of a dog is most important. Once the dogs are in the show they may not be taken off their benches for more than 15 minutes at a time just enough to allow them to be taken to the 'dogs loo' which is a huge ring with sawdust. They have to be on their benches because people pay to go to Crufts to see the dogs and if they were not on their benches it wouldn't be fair to those who come long distances or short distances for that matter to see the best dogs in the world or so we believe.

The Obedience ring is a very popular one. You can only enter a dog for the Crufts obedience if it has qualified by winning a Challenge Certificate for the dog with the best marks at a Championship Show, and this takes some doing.

Most trainers seem to like Border Collies or German Shepherd Dogs (formerly called Alsatians) as they are very willing workers and easy to train. I would like to see more breeds entered. You can almost hear a pin drop when one of the obedience dogs is doing a difficult exercise like finding the piece of cloth that has only the judges scent on it. When the exercise is completed the whole place resounds with cheering.

If you have never seen Crufts, it is well worth a visit although people say their feet ache after a day spent there as you have to stand up all day and the crowds are enormous. But it is a day you will never forget, even if you don't own a dog.

*Left:* Two types of Goldfish, 'veiltail' (left) and 'telescope-fantail' (right). *Right:* The most common, if not necessarily the best, home for goldfish kept in the house.

## Goldfish

Although they live in the water, goldfish need oxygen which they 'breathe' by taking water which contains air, into their mouths, and passing it through their gills. The wider the fish tank, the more air the water can keep absorbing. This is why a narrow-necked bowl is quite the wrong shape. An oblong-shaped tank has a bigger surface area of water and is much the best choice.

Fine aquarium gravel should be bought from a pet shop, first washed in several changes of water, then placed in a tank to a depth of about 4 cms. Place the tank in a light place, but not directly in the sun's rays, or the water may become too warm and lose oxygen.

The tank should also be quite level and it helps to get it exactly right if you stand it on several sheets of newspaper or a piece of foam. To fill the tank, place a sheet of newspaper on the gravel and pour on the water, very slowly. In this way the gravel will stay level and will not be swirled around. Use rain-water, or tap water which has been standing for a day or two.

Some water plants, again from the pet shop, will decorate the tank and help to keep the water fresh. Then a cover of glass, plastic or wood should be placed over the top, slightly raised by a small piece of cork glued to each corner of the tank. This will keep dust out, but allow air to circulate over the water. It will also stop any very lively fish jumping right out of the tank!

Do not put too many goldfish into the water and make sure they are all the same size. A tank measuring about 60 cms long x 30 cms wide x 30 cms deep will take four fish 8 cms long.

Dry food from the pet shop is the easiest way to feed the fish, but they will only need a pinch of food each day. Do not give them more than they can clear up within about five minutes, or it will just decay in the water.

A quarter of the water should be changed every week; siphoning it off and removing any sediment in the tank. Before pouring in the fresh water, use a thermometer to make sure that it is practically the same temperature as that already in the tank.

Goldfish usually swim around well below the surface, but if they start swimming near the top, gasping and blowing bubbles, they are probably short of oxygen. This sometimes happens in warm weather, and the remedy is to change some of the water again.

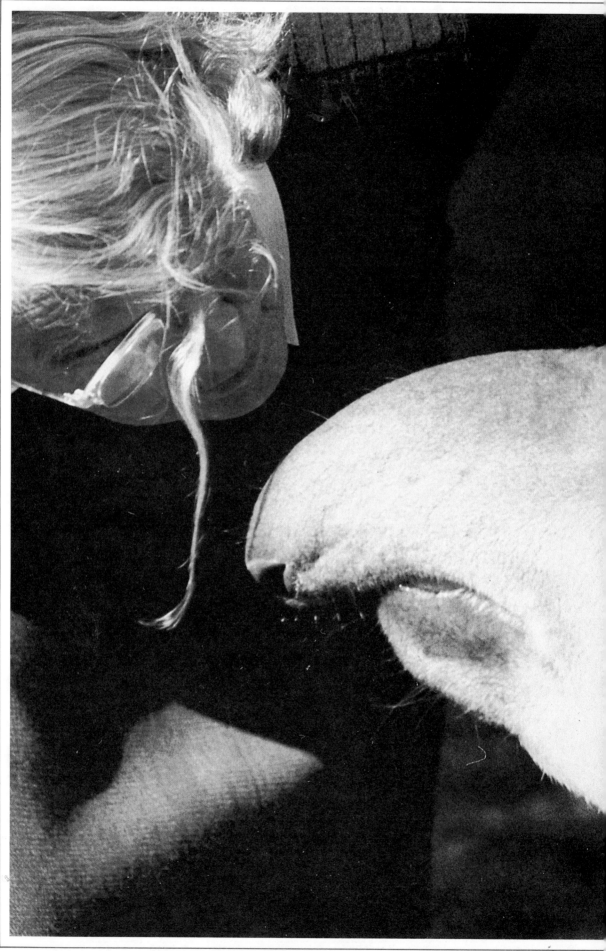

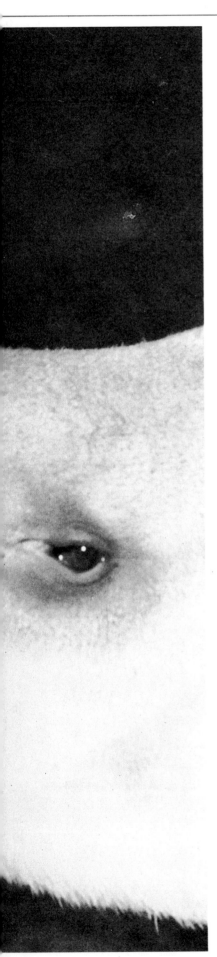

# The Breathing Up Trick

This isn't a conjuring trick, this is a "how do you do" in horse language. It was taught to me many years ago in South America by an old Guarani Indian whose tribe used it to break in their horses without fear.

It is done by placing your hand behind your back and gently breathing down your nose towards the horse. Stand quite still and the horse will usually hear this breathing and recognise it as coming from a friend. If another horse does it they will breathe up each other's noses and then stay with each other as friends.

If you do it to an unbroken horse it will want to be with you all the time unless you are cruel to it. I have never known a horse do anything nasty to me if I have given it this greeting. In fact I reckon to saddle it up and get on its back in a few minutes and as long as you teach it kindly what you want from it, it will remain your friend.

Recently I wanted to see if this nose to nose greeting was shared by any other kind of animal so I went to Woburn Zoo and got permission to try it out on the Giraffes, although the public

*Barbara demonstrates her now famous 'breathing-up trick' with* left: *a Collared Peccary and* above: *A Hyena. Both animals responded.*

are not allowed to get out of their cars normally. It worked. The Giraffe's great head bent down to my nose and not only breathed a welcome but gave me a huge lick with it's pink tongue which was very rough like a cow's.

I went to other Giraffes and each one acknowledged my greeting in the same way. I found the Bongo antelopes did it, the Tapirs at Dudley Zoo and the Hyenas and Llamas and Collared Peccaries liked it, but Wolves and birds didn't respond at all.

Most deer treat it as a threat rather than a welcome and the stag will often stamp his foot to warn his wives to stay away from this queer human being who blows down her nose instead of bringing them food.

The trouble with trying out the breathing trick is that most of the animals are used to human beings so it is not the first greeting with a human which it is meant to be.

Cattle love it and give deep blows back to your nose. Try it through a fence and see if the heifers will come up to you. Then you will have learnt the Guarani Indian trick from South America.

Barbara has found that her 'breathing-up trick' can work with both wild animals (small pic) and domesticated animals.

# Pet's Corner

## Birds

Of all the birds which are kept as pets the budgerigar is the most popular, because it is easy to look after and costs very little to feed. But budgies do like company and if your pet is to be left on its own for hours, during the daytime, then it is better to buy two for company. Not two hen birds, though, as these are unlikely to make good friends. Choose either a cock and hen, or two cock birds, if they are to live happily together.

If you want to teach your budgie to talk, it is best to choose one between six and nine weeks old. A young bird will have bars or narrow stripe markings across the front of its head and flecks on the lower part of the face. The fleshy part at the base of the beak, called the cere, is purplish in young cocks and bluish-white in young hens.

Both will become talkers if you spend a lot of time teaching them, although males generally make better talkers than females. Older birds are more difficult to teach and in some cases will never learn. It is also best to keep a talking budgie on its own, although it has been known for one budgie to teach another.

When you bring your new pet home, let him get used to his new surroundings for a couple of days. Then you can start coming closer to his cage, saying quietly a simple word or two, like 'pretty boy' or perhaps the bird's name.

Once he is more used to you, start training him to hop onto your finger. Slowly reach into the cage, talking softly. Put your index finger next to his perch, raising it under his breast until he

hops onto it. Move him gently to another perch, but do not take him out of the cage for some days, by which time he should be used to perching on your finger.

Keep talking to him, saying the same words over and over, until he at last starts repeating them. You will have to be very patient, for it will probably take six weeks or more, before he starts 'talking'. How much he learns to say depends on how clever your budgie is, and how much time you spend with him.

The cage in which you keep your budgie should give him plenty of space to flutter around and although he will enjoy having some toys, like a mirror, bell or tiny ladder, don't clutter up the cage with too many of these things.

Ideally, the cage should

29

be placed opposite a window, where it will have plenty of light, but not so that the sun shines onto it. Don't raise it higher than 120 cms (about 4 ft) off the floor and make sure it is well away from any draughts, especially from doorways. At night the cage should be covered with a piece of light-weight cloth, so that your pet can get all the beauty sleep he needs.

Every week, clean the cage, feeding pots and toys with water which contains a small amount of household disinfectant, and re-line the floor with a fresh piece of sand sheet.

Don't, of course, leave doors or windows open when you let your budgie fly around the room, and do make sure that an open fire-place is completely covered with a piece of board or a fireguard, or he'll be up the chimney and away. Put a cloth over any mirrors and a piece of net across the window, so that the budgie does

not try to fly through the glass and injure himself. He may want to take too close an interest in house plants, so cover them up or remove them while he's exploring the room. Don't forget, always put the cat out first.

It may be difficult to get your budgie back into the cage, at first, so you may have to use an old hat or a newspaper 'cone' to capture him. First darken the room by drawing the curtains, then use a torch to find him. Slip your thumb and fore-finger each side of his head and clasp the wings close to his body, then pop him gently back into the cage. Later he should learn to go back on his own, even when you tell him to, if he is very obedient.

A budgie's main food should be canary seed and millet, with occasional tit-bits like spray millet, chick-weed, lettuce, apple or carrot. Keep seed-pots filled every day, first blowing off the empty husks that he will

leave on top. Make sure he has some budgerigar grit, cuttlebone and fresh drink-ing water always available. Give him a small amount of green food two or three mornings each week, well washed and drained, and remove any that is left un-eaten at the end of the day.

Looked after this way your budgerigar, which is really a small, Australian Parakeet, will stay healthy. If he feels unwell his eyes will look dull and he will become much less active. He will fluff up his feathers and probably huddle in the corner of his cage. In this case, take him to the vet as soon as possible.

Ask the vet's advice if his beak or claws should be-come overgrown, and when he is moulting, it helps to give water mixed half and half with cow's milk. If the budgie seems 'naughty' and starts to chew the furniture, put a small block of softwood or twig from a fruit tree in his cage.

In the wild, the budgerigar is bright grass green with yellow on the head and wings, but an enormous number of different coloured budgies have been bred from tame birds, so you will have to decide which is your favourite. Apart from this, the best choice is a quiet bird, but one with alert, bright eyes.

The Cockatiel is another delightful little Australian bird which is now being imported in larger numbers. About twice the size of a budgie, it needs much the same care and treatment, and makes a very good first pet for a young boy or girl.

It has a cockatoo-like crest and softly coloured feathers, brighter in the adult male which has a pale yellow head and neck with a brick-red spot on each cheek. The body is mainly grey with black and white markings. In the female the crest is grey and the body colouring generally softer. The young cock birds look very much like the hens in colouring, until they are two years old.

Unlike the budgie, the cockatiel has a quiet voice and makes pleasing, whistling notes. Although it is unlikely to learn more than a few simple words, if kept on its own it becomes very tame and friendly.

There is a large family of bigger parrots and although they are expensive to buy, many of them are kept as pets. But a parrot should be chosen very carefully and you need to have a great deal of expert advice before deciding on one of these as a pet. The African grey parrot is the most popular and makes the best talker, but it really needs the care of an older person who has kept birds for a long time and understands a lot about them.

For the same reason the Mynah bird, although a very good talker, is not really suitable for a young person's

*Left:* A Border Canary, clear yellow hen, wiping her face on perch among Cotoneaster berries. *Above:* Yellow-throated Mynah at drinking pool.

pet. It needs lots of attention, plenty of room – and it is a messy eater. Each bird has its own personality, and needs a very understanding owner to be able to lead a happy life.

On the other hand, the Canary has simple needs, very much like the budgie, except that it is not normally let out of its cage. Unlike the budgie, too, the canary enjoys a bath, and a container of water for this purpose should be hung on the cage two or three times a week. It should always be removed before mid-day though, so that the bird can dry off before bedtime.

It is also better to give a canary a long cage, rather than a dome-shaped or square one, so that it will have more space to fly.

All cock canaries sing well, but the best is the Roller canary, while the Border, Gloucester and Red-factor are other favourites.

Jackdaws, Magpies and Jays used to be kept as pets, as they are very clever mimics and could often be taught to imitate the human voice. These days, though, it is against the law to cage any British wild bird, unless it is found sick or injured. When it is well again, it must then be released.

Special names are given to the homes of some animals and birds. Can you answer these questions?

1. A squirrel lives in a snug nest built in a fork or hollow of a tree. What is it called?

2. A badger tunnels into a bank or mound of earth and is very particular about keeping his home clean. Can you give it a name?

3. A hole in the bank of a river is the otter's choice. Do you know what it is called?

4. Rooks build noisily every Spring, often repairing old nests in a group high in the tree tops. What do people call this cluster of nests?

5. The hare makes do with no more than a hollow in the ground which is called a . . . .?

Cows come in herds and sheep in flocks, but there are different names for other groups of animals, birds and fish.

a. The lion likes to live in a small group or 'family'. This is called a . . . . .?

b. Wolves hunt together in a . . . .

c. On the ground, geese gather in a flock, but wild geese can sometimes be seen flying in a 'V' shape. This is a . . . . . of geese.

d. You may have only seen a herring on a plate, but fishermen might see them in a . . . . .

e. Porpoises may swim around in small or large numbers. Any of these groups can be called a . . . . . .

*Answers on page 63*

# The Joy of Owning a Pony

For most boys and girls, a pony of their own is just a dream. First, a pony needs plenty of room in a field, paddock or orchard. A hardy animal can go through the winter without a stable, although a simple three-sided shelter with a roof should be built for it, so that the pony can stand out of the wind and rain if it chooses.

If you haven't a piece of ground large enough for a pony to live, does it mean that all the fun of riding is not for you ? By no means. Many young people are now able to ride regularly, in both the town and country, as more stables offer riding and lessons 'by the hour'.

Wherever you live there are almost bound to be riding schools and stables within a short distance, and one way to find them is to look in the Yellow Pages of the telephone directory.

If you are a beginner it is a very good idea to have a look at the place you have chosen before you go ahead with any lessons. See how well the ponies are turned out and how carefully the riding instructor looks after his – or her – pupils, especially if they are moving along the road.

There are also residential centres where you can spend your holidays learning to ride, and advertisements in the popular riding magazines will help you find these places.

Once you can ride reasonably well and safely, then pony trekking during the holidays is another way to enjoy the company of ponies, and for really experienced and older riders there is trail riding, when you can canter, gallop and jump over miles of countryside.

All this does, of course, cost quite a lot. So if you are pony-mad but have only a little pocket-money, the best way to get amongst ponies is to make friends with people who stable a number of animals, and see if you can persuade them to let you ride sometimes. A farmer may have ponies which he stables for week-end riders and these may need exercise during the week. Go to the local pony shows where you may find riders who are glad to have someone hold their ponies while they grab a Coke and sandwich from

the refreshment tent. Or you may be able to persuade your parents to try a farmhouse holiday next time, making sure the farmer does keep ponies, or that there are stables nearby.

First of all, though, learn all you can about the care of ponies. For instance, they need careful feeding and how much food they are given depends on whether they are working hard or just being ridden occasionally. A hard-working pony will need a carefully measured quantity of good hay, good oats and bran every day. Fresh water, too, is most important and a pony must have time to digest anything he eats and drinks before he starts working, or he may end up with colic, which is a very bad tummy ache indeed.

A stabled pony needs head to tail grooming daily, and this is an important part

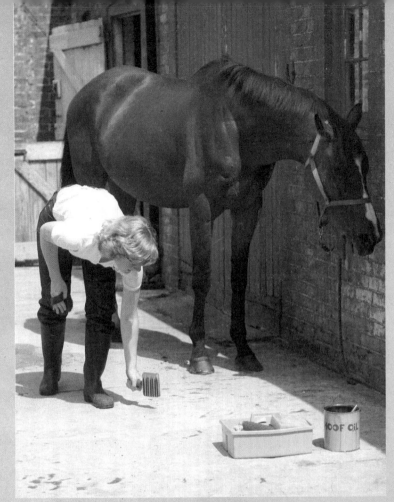

*Main pic:* New Forest Ponies at drinking pool. These are one of the traditional breed of pony and are ideal for learning to ride on.
*Above:* Grooming is an essential exercise when looking after a horse. Here a young stable girl cleans her curry comb by tapping it on the ground.

of the serious horse-lover's education. You must learn to use a dandy brush and curry comb correctly, 'pull' or comb out untidy hair in the mane and tail, wash, bandage and plait the pony's mane, examine its feet and oil the hooves.

The pony's health has to be cared for, and you must watch all the time for any coughing, shivering, itching, hot feet or accidental scratches. These are all signs that he needs care and attention, and although you may be able to give the minor treatments yourself, you must know when to bring in the vet, or possibly the smithy.

It is just as important to keep the stables spotlessly clean and there is a right and wrong way to do most things, even to strewing the straw for the pony's bed. This should be tossed in the air, so that it falls in all directions, to make a more comfortable bedding, and piled round the edge of the stable to prevent draughts.

Tack, which covers all the leather equipment including saddle and bridle, must be looked after to keep it clean, supple and well preserved. Leather should be sponged clean after use, treated with saddle soap and polished with a soft cloth.

It is necessary to saddle and bridle the pony correctly. The rein is placed over his head before slipping the bit into his mouth and lifting the bridle into place over his ears. The saddle should fit the pony's back comfortably and the girth – the buckled strap that holds the saddle in place – needs to be tightened so that just two fingers can be slipped between the girth and the pony's body.

Not least, there are your own riding clothes. A hard cap or hat is essential, to protect your head in case you are thrown. Shoes or

*Above:* How to comb a horse's main. *Right:* Pony competitors wait to enter the ring.

jodhpur boots can be chosen, but not rubber-soled shoes as these might cling to the stirrup-iron if you fall. Apart from this, it really depends when and where you are riding, how well turned out you need to be. However, trousers or jodhpurs should not be too tight, especially round the knee, and there must also be plenty of room between the seat and the knee, if you are to ride comfortably. If you wear a riding coat, however old, it will look smart if you make sure that it is long enough to cover your seat, and to finish your outfit, string gloves look right and feel comfortable.

If you are just starting to ride, then a well-trained, experienced and patient pony is the ideal mount. Maybe one of the traditional breeds such as the Shetland, Welsh, Exmoor, Dartmoor or New Forest ponies.

The Shetland is still the purest strain and is very much in demand as a child's mount. Some of the moorland ponies have been cross-bred, deliberately or accidentally, but the basic toughness of the semi-wild pony allows it to withstand the worst of weathers. Some have been cross-bred with the fleet-footed Arab, and these can usually be recognised by the neat head

and elegant neck which is typical of the beautiful Arab horses.

If, so far, you have only been able to admire ponies from a distance, there are a few basic rules which everyone has to understand. First, never approach a pony suddenly, or from the rear. Talk to it softly as you come near it, so that it knows you are coming closer. Of course, many friendly ponies simply ask for attention, but don't expect them all to act like this with strangers.

If you are offering a tit-bit, always place the lump of sugar or apple with fingers stretched back and thumb tucked firmly against and towards the back of the hand. *Never* offer the pony a 'bunch of fingers' because he can't see your hand close to his mouth and sort out fingers from food. Give him the tit-bit the correct way and his teeth will just slide harmlessly over your palm.

Watch those back legs, too, because these are the pony's defence weapons. Even the mildest-mannered pony may lash out suddenly, maybe because he's startled or the flies are tormenting him.

His ears will show whether he's nervous or suspicious by being well tucked back. Pricked forward, they show that he is relaxed. If his head is raised at the same time he's very alert and listening–perhaps to the sound of another pony trotting along the road. If he paws the ground with one front hoof, he's feeling impatient–especially if he sees other ponies doing something which he can't, for the moment, join in.

Many ponies have a great sense of fun and most love company, both animal and human. So you can learn a great deal by just watching them and getting to know the way they think and feel, which is the best preparation you can have before learning to ride and maybe, one day, owning your very own pony.

# Pet's Corner

*Left:* Red Tabby Longhair cat and kitten. *Right:* Ginger farm kitten playing in straw.

## Cats

A cat likes to do very much as it pleases, but if it is treated well it will become a very loving pet. A she-cat or 'queen' is usually very patient and will accept a lot of handling, although there will be times when she decides she's had quite enough and will take refuge on top of a cupboard or other high place.

Cats can be trained not to do certain things, like choosing to sleep on the best bed, jumping on the table or climbing the curtains. If a kitten does anything against the rules, remove it quickly with a very firm 'no! It will soon learn how far it can go, so don't be tempted to let it get away with a piece of mischief 'just this once'.

In return, do make sure your new pet has a comfortable bed in a place away from any draught, and where it can rest peacefully without being disturbed. A strong cardboard box lined with newspapers or cast-off 'woollies' will do well, or you might like to buy a wicker or strong plastic 'basket' from the pet shop.

A cat should also be provided with a 'scratching post', ideally a piece of bark-covered wood on which it can sharpen its claws. This will help to stop unpopular habits like scratching paintwork or a favourite rose tree.

When you first bring your kitten home it should, ideally, be eight weeks old. From six weeks onwards it will have been eating solid food and from the age of seven or eight weeks it should be fed small meals at least three times a day. By the time it is six months old, two meals a day is the usual arrangement, one in the morning and one in the evening, with small saucers of milk put down at the same time.

Some cats become very fussy about their food, and so it is a good idea to offer yours plenty of variety. Lightly cooked meat, dry or tinned cat food and a little bread, potatoes or cereal can be tried. A little green vegetable is good for a cat, if it will eat this, especially if there is no garden in which it can find grass to chew. In this case, it is also a good idea to plant some mixed grass seed in a pot or box, so that your pet can take a little when it wants some.

If you feed chicken or fish to your cat, make sure the bones are removed first, and whatever food you put down, remove the dishes as soon as the meal is over. Most cats love a saucer of milk, but don't leave half-full bowls around for your pet to drink later, as milk quickly goes stale. Water should be placed where it can be reached any time and some cats enjoy drinking water from under a dripping tap.

Cats are very clean by nature and will quickly learn to use a soil tray or 'ask' to be let out into the garden when necessary. A cat also washes itself thoroughly, cleaning its fur with its rough tongue. In doing this, it also swallows a lot of hair, and it will help both the cat and the carpet if you groom your pet regularly, using a cat comb and brush. If you start doing this when he (or she) is a kitten, he will enjoy it, but be very gentle and give up when the cat 'tells you' he has had enough. (Long-haired cats are more of a problem, as their hair can get very matted without regular attention, so think twice about this before falling for an adorable 'fluffy ball' of a kitten).

Cats are usually very healthy pets, but they should be inoculated against feline enteritis. The first injection is usually given at six to eight weeks old and the second when the kitten is twelve weeks old. After that an injection each year will keep it safe from this killer disease.

You can also have your pet vaccinated against 'cat flu'. This produces all the signs of a very bad cold, with sneezing, and running eyes and nose. Also watch out for ear infections or an abscess in the ear, when the cat will keep shaking its head and scratching its ears. These are cases for the vet to see.

Many people now have their cats neutered by the vet, so that they do not produce unwanted kittens. But kittens are great fun to watch as they grow up, and if you are sure there will be good homes waiting for them later, you may want your cat to have at least one 'family'.

When a cat is expecting kittens (whether you have arranged for her to meet a male or 'tom' of the same breed, or she has found a mate in the neighbourhood), she will need extra food, which should be gradually increased over the next nine weeks. After the kittens are born, she will need several feeds a day and should be offered plenty of milk.

Just before the kittens are born the cat will become restless and will seek the best 'nest' possible in which to have her young. Her first choice is most likely to be the softest feather quilt she can find, but she should be firmly removed from this and given a comfortable nursery of her own. Again, a box lined with newspapers or soft, warm fabric is suitable.

Let her stay as quiet as possible, both before and after the kittens are born. If she has too many people fussing around the tiny kittens, she will remove them to a place of safety where it might be difficult to find them.

The kittens, born blind, will open their eyes in nine or ten days. They will then

*Left:* Black Shorthair Cat and *above:* European Shorthair Cat — spotted.

begin to explore the outside world beyond their 'nursery', a little at a time, until they are ready to find a new home and begin life as someone else's special pet.

You may choose a tabby, a black or ginger-coloured cat, or very likely one with any of these markings combined with white. Curiously, all-white cats with blue eyes are usually deaf, but those with green or yellow eyes are not, while a tortoiseshell cat is almost always a female. Sometimes you may see a Manx cat with no tail and long hind legs.

Siamese cats are very popular and in some ways they behave more like a dog, taking walks with their owners and each being very devoted to one person. These cats have cream-coloured bodies and dark brown or chocolate coloured head, legs and tail, or another type has a white coat with greyish-blue markings or 'points'. Siamese cats, like other pure breeds cost a lot more to buy than the ordinary puss, which may well be offered free to a good home. And if you give a cat a good home, it will soon become a contented member of the family.

Picture by kind permission of ICI Paint Division.

# Training The Dulux Dog

I am sure you all love the big Old English Sheepdog who does the Dulux paint commercial, and perhaps wonder how he is trained to do the clever things he does in some of them.

Perhaps you have met one of these dogs sitting majestically in shops whilst the children and grown ups pat him. Very often he will be sitting on a table so his paws don't get trodden on in the crowd that collects to talk to him.

The training of the future Dulux dog usually starts when the puppy is about eight weeks old. But a recent puppy came for his three half hour lessons when he was only six weeks old and he was very clever. I only gave him three half hour lessons and he learnt to sit and stay where he was told to stay. He ran to the paint tin when told and jumped up with his front feet on the tin, then he learnt to bark, jump off and go off the stage. As well as this he learnt to pick up his feeding dish and hold it because sometimes the dog has to hold a paint tin for an advertisement and to learn to pick up something when told is getting him ready to do films or television. When the dog does right he gets a tit-bit and lots of love.

The Dulux dogs have to learn everything by obeying my voice as they have so much hair over their eyes they cannot see very well, and they often bump into things. When actually giving them a lesson I pin the hair back off the eyes with a hair clip, so the dog can see where my voice comes from and where I am standing.

Recently I have trained the latest dog to do the commercials he is called "Duke" and is five years old, rather older than the other dogs I trained. He was very easy to train and learnt to obey my voice so quickly that when on one day I could not be at the studios to work him his master was able to take my place by using a tape recorder on which I had put the instructions to the dog. It was, I am told, quite funny to see how quickly he obeyed my voice much to the delight of the film director.

Big dogs get very hot and tired with all the hot lights on a film set, so Duke had to be taken out into the air very often and he had a fan in his rest room to keep him cool. If he got too hot he panted a lot and then his hair got very wet and it turns brown when wet, so has to be dried with a towel or hair dryer and then have talcum powder rubbed into it to make him as beautiful as possible. He has a bath the day before the shooting of the film and is brushed every time before the camera films him.

Lots of people want to pat him but this is not allowed in the film studio or the dog gets too tired.

Duke is not fed before he works because he gets tit bits as rewards or when he has to go with children or grown ups somewhere they give him a Polo Mint at first so he knows where to go.

He has learnt to have a drink from his rest room basin by standing up on his hind legs and balancing on the basin with his front legs.

While a baby cat is a kitten and a young dog is a puppy, other animals and birds have special names before they are fully grown.

1. Some people keep goats, like cows, for their milk, and children are sometimes nick-named after the young goats. What are they called?

2. A donkey likes company, animals and human, and is not so 'stupid' as people may think. Can you remember what a young one is called?

3. A roe deer is a gentle and loving mother and will not move far from her young. The mother is a doe and she usually has twins which are —?

4. When bears are born they are very tiny and spend the first few weeks of their lives snuggled up to their mother while she finishes her long winter sleep. Then she brings her . . . . into the open.

5. An 'aunt' elephant often helps to look after the young one, which is called a . . . .?

Animals are placed in special groups for different reasons even though they may not look at all alike. For instance:-

a. Both the horse and deer are *ungulates*. What does this mean?

b. The kangaroo and the Australian ring-tailed possum are *marsupials*. What makes them different from most other animals?

c. The owl and the bat are *nocturnal* creatures. When would you expect to find them flying around?

d. Dogs and cats are *carnivores*. What puts them in this group?

e. The horse and the sheep are *herbivorous*. What do they have in common?

*Answers* on page 63

# 'How I tamed a Praying Mantis'

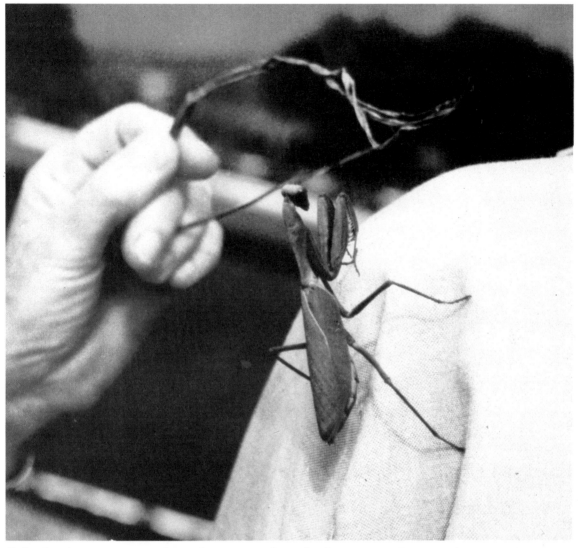

I don't suppose many of you have ever heard of or seen a Praying Mantis. They look like giant grasshoppers and live in the tropics.

I was on a trip in Gambia when we went up into the mountains to see a reservoir, and all the tourists were standing on a large strip of concrete, when the large green Praying Mantis ran out of the grass nearby and was dashing hither and thither terrified of the tourists.

The tourists wished to photograph it but of course it would not stay still. So jokingly I said to the people 'If you will all stand still I'll train it for you'.

I used the tone of voice I use to dogs. I said 'Si-it' and 'stay'. The Mantis stopped running about and looked at me. I then said 'sit up and bring your feet up, the people want to photograph you'. The Praying Mantis obeyed me. But the people said it didn't show up on concrete so could I pick it up and put it on a white coat one of the tourists was wearing.

So confidently I said 'yes of course', bent down and gently picked it up and put it on the coat. Again I told it to sit and bring its feet up higher, which it obeyed.

They all took pictures and I asked them if they'd finished as the bus driver wanted to go on and they said they had, so I told the Praying Mantis to 'hop it' and off it jumped to the ground and ran away.

I wonder what it told other Praying Mantis about that funny lady.

# Pet's Corner

*Left:* The most common type of tortoise kept as pets and *right:* Spur-thighed tortoise.

## Tortoises

It is important to pick a healthy tortoise for a pet and the first thing to look for, when making your choice, is one which is actively moving around. The shell should not be cracked and it should be more than 10 cms long, otherwise the tortoise will be too young to hibernate and keeping it through the winter will be a lot of trouble. When picked up, the tortoise will probably pull in its head and kick with its hind legs, maybe making a small hissing noise at the same time.

When you get home, put your new pet in a shallow bowl of just-warm water and leave it for a few minutes. While taking this bath it will probably drink some of the water, which will also freshen the mouth and eyes, besides cleaning the shell.

Make a home for the tortoise, using a strong box, with the floor raised a little from the ground. It should have an entrance in one side and a waterproof roof. Inside, the floor should be covered with a thick layer of straw,

dry leaves or hay.

This box can then be placed inside an enclosure measuring at least 250 cms by 125 cms, with boarded sides about 25 cms high.

A tortoise, however, prefers to roam around and will do its best to get out into the world if it has a chance. If it can be allowed the freedom of the garden it will be very happy, but unless it is walled in, the tortoise probably won't stay put. It will burrow under or squeeze through most barriers, so you may only be able to let it out while there is someone around to watch it.

A tortoise likes lettuce, spinach, carrot tops, the leaves and flowers of dandilions, clover, buttercups, plantains and peas. Some like tomatoes, apples, pears, plums and strawberries, while others become fond of bread and milk. Leaves of various kinds should form its main food, but it can be offered as varied a vegetarian diet as possible, to find out which things it likes best.

A tortoise can only drink from a shallow bowl and may upset a deeper one. But it does enjoy a bath. A large, shallow pan sunk into the earth, with the rim level with the ground, is ideal.

A very important part of keeping a tortoise is making arrangements for it to go into its winter hibernation. In the autumn, as the weather gets colder, the tortoise will become lazy and sleepy. It should then be given a wooden box filled with dry leaves or straw. Tuck the tortoise carefully into this, cover the top with several thicknesses of sacking or cloth and place it in a cool but frost-proof place. A garden shed or garage may be suitable, but not a warm cupboard or heated room.

When spring comes round, and its long winter sleep is over, the tortoise should be given a warm bath and its eyes bathed with boric lotion. It may not want food at first, but if kept warm at night it will soon liven up and become active again.

# Is Your Dog Naughty?

Q. Every time I groom my dog it bites me. What shall I do?

A. Put on a very thick overcoat, and a thick pair of leather gloves. Hold the dog lightly by its choke chain and start to groom it, using a cheerful and excited tone of voice to hold its interest. I always say, 'Who's going to have a lovely grooming?' By the tone of my voice the dog thinks grooming is something most exciting and stands still. Should he attempt to bite, give him a quick, sharp jerk in a downward direction on any type of thick choke chain and the command 'Leave'. Carry on grooming, as his bites cannot hurt you through the gloves. In no time at all he will learn that it is better to stand still and get praise.

Be sure you use the right sort of grooming implements for the breed of dog. If the dog has long hair, use a wire hair brush after the style of the Maison Pearson brushes for human beings. If you have a Poodle, you will need a wire comb.

But if the dog has a short smooth coat use a glove brush, which is incidentally further protection for your hand.

Q. Should I let my dog play with other people's dogs when they meet out on a walk? When doing so he will not come when called.

A. By all means let your dog have fun with others, provided always that you ask permission from the owner if the other dog is accompanied. But all dogs should be trained to leave others alone instantly on command and return to their owner. This is achieved by putting your dog on a long cord attached to a choke chain. Should the dog not come when called, give the command 'Come' and simultaneously give a really sharp tug on the cord, hard enough to face the dog towards you. If it is done quickly, no harm whatsoever comes to the dog, except that it gets a shock at being made to return to you against its will. Directly the dog faces you, call it again with a very loving voice and praise it. If it still doesn't come, continue the short quick jerks until it reaches you.

You must employ the right tone of voice; firm when the dog is disobeying and very loving when it makes any attempt to come. Most dogs soon prefer the praise. Nowadays you can buy a retractable lead that runs out to 10 metres and coils itself back into its holder. Called Flexi, it is very useful for dogs that won't come when called or bitches on heat.

Q. My dog screams and barks in the car even if we are there. What can I do to stop it?

A. Teach him daily to lie down on command, and stay lying down until you give him permission to get up. To do this you must pull firmly on the choke chain under his chin until his chin rests on the ground; a quick push on his back with the other hand soon puts him down. Repeat as often as he attempts to get up. At first it will be a battle of wills. You must win, for a dog lying down cannot bark for any length of time.

When he has learnt this at home graduate to the car. When in your car run a long string from his choke chain down to the floor and under the seat-belt anchorage and up over the passenger's shoulder. Should he get up he can be pulled to the down.

Q. My dog barks at all our friends when they visit us, and recently has started to bite them if they move quickly. Shall I banish her to another room?

A. You must never banish your dog to another room or you will admit defeat. If you have a brave friend or two, give them overcoats and thick gloves, and take your dog up to them and make her stand while they caress her. Use loving and comforting words all the time. If she attempts to bite, give a sharp jerk on the choke chain and use a very cross voice. Praise her all the time she is being caressed by your friend. Then send her to her basket with the command 'Down stay' and see that she obeys.

A lot of people don't like dogs anyway, and you should never embarrass your friends with your dog's unwanted attentions. An indoor kennel is really the answer and these can be bought. They can fold up for travelling or when not in use.

Q. My dog puddles on the floor directly I bring it indoors, however long it has been out. What can I do to house train it ?

A. Make or buy an indoor kennel for it and if it has not performed as required outside, pop it into this kennel. The kennel can be made like a rabbit hutch and have a blanket at one end and sand or turf at the other. At frequent intervals take the dog out to its same grassy spot and repeat the command you have chosen to use when you wish it to be clean.

Directly he does obey, love him and praise him so that he knows he has been good.

Q. My dog barks all day, running up and down our garden fence, and is annoying the neighbours. What can I do to stop him ?

A. This question always amazes me. Why leave a dog in the garden alone to be bored and therefore naughty and noisy ? What is there for him to do ? There are no rats or rabbits to chase, he must not dig up the flower beds, so he does the next best thing, barks defiance at all who pass by.

The answer is to take your dog into the house with you where he belongs, and exercise him with you. Once he has got accustomed to your constant companionship he will soon forget about barking in the garden. Turning your dog out is laziness on your part.

Q. How do I teach my dog not to take food from strangers ?

A. Ask your friends to offer the dog food when they come to the house. As he goes to take it, whip your hand in front of his nose and give the command 'Leave'. Repeat as often as he goes to take the food. Directly he turns his head away praise him, and give him the food yourself.

Q. My dog is getting old and makes himself offensive in the room so often that I am always apologising for whiffs and having to open the window. Is there anything I can do to stop this, or must I banish him from the room ?

A. Big dogs especially suffer in this way.

Cut out all fat from his diet and give him vitamin A. Charcoal helps enormously and can be bought in biscuit form. Never banish a dog for something he cannot help. A sensitive dog would suffer greatly at being parted from you.

Q. My dog pulls my arms out when I take him out. I have tried smacking him and holding a stick in front of his nose, but he still continues to pull. Please give me some advice.

A. Buy a correct choke chain which is thick-lined, and a four-foot lead. Hold the dog on the left-hand side, with the lead held very loosely in the right hand. Directly the dog forges ahead, give the command 'heel' and a sharp firm downward jerk across your knees. Immediately praise the dog. If your jerks are sharp enough, the dog will stop this pulling. You cannot hurt a dog with sharp jerks, but remember gentle pulls are ineffective and choke the dog, which is unkind.

Q. My dog will chase all livestock. How can I cure him ? Sheep chasing is his particular joy.

A. Under no circumstances must you allow your dog to be free near livestock. The only real cure I know for sheep chasing is one used in the Argentine, but no dog lover would like to inflict it on his dog. They muzzle the dog, tie him down in a gateway and chase a flock of sheep over him. The sheep jump over him without hurting him in any way, but the fright he gets cures him for ever. They say, of course, that a fierce ram will attack a dog and put the fear of sheep into him, but I am doubtful if there is a cure. Keep your dog on a retractable Flexi lead when near livestock.

Q. My dog eats filth. What can I do to cure this ?

A. This is a dietary deficiency, or means that the dog may have worms or lacks mineral or trace elements. Get him treated for worms first, and then see that he has a balanced diet with plenty of vitamins. I use Vionate from Polliome Ltd., 7 York Street, Twickenham, Middlesex.

# Teaching Your Dog Tricks

I AM always being asked by young owners how to teach their dogs tricks. Well, this is how I teach mine.

First you must have enormous patience for if you lose your temper you won't get anywhere. Next you must never overtire your dog. If it does something right first time, praise it and leave the trick. Be sure never to teach a dog a trick without giving it some reward, either in food, or abundant play, and of course shower it with love and admiration when it has done right. A dog adores being clever for its owner and your voice will tell it how pleased you are . Lastly, never bore your dog, and by that I mean don't keep making it do an old trick all the time and don't make it show off time and time again to your friends. Teach it new things. And above all never laugh at a dog unkindly. They are very sensitive to this and hate ridicule in any form.

Tricks should always be developed from something the dog naturally likes doing, for then not only will you and your friends enjoy watching, but your dog will have fun doing them.

Here are a few tricks you might like to teach your dog.

### Picking her name out of the alphabet

You will want the twenty-six letters of the alphabet painted in black on both sides of strong cardboard squares, so that the audience can see them clearly. Keep the letters JUNO (the letters will of course vary according to your dog's name) in one bag and all the others in another. They must never be mixed. Next, set them in a circle on the floor, but get a friend to put down the ones without the dog's name on them so that you never touch them, because this trick is done by the dog picking out the letters bearing your scent. Add the letters JUNO to the rest, keeping them widely spaced so that the dog has to look for them. Now take the dog on her lead to the letters and point to lots of them in turn. When you find one bearing one of her letters say 'Good girl' and make her pick it up and bring it to you. Continue backwards and forwards until she has found them all with your help. Praise her a lot. When she has done this a few times, she will know that it is the cardboard with your scent that gets the praise and reward, and will soon rush up and select the right ones. It doesn't matter in what order they are found as long as you hold them up in the right order for the audience to see at the end. Few people guess how this trick is done.

### Counting

First teach your dog to bark on command. I either bang the door knocker or the kitchen table and say 'speak' in a most excited tone of voice. The dog barks and gets meat as a reward. Soon it will bark without the bang on the table or knocker simply on the command 'speak'. Now begin blinking hard when you say 'speak' and hold the reward up high so that the dog watches your face. Blink once at first, then twice, and eventually blink every time you want the dog to bark. Quickly the dog picks up the connection between the reward and the blink, and will go on barking until you stop blinking and stare him in the face. When you ask him what two and two make you blink four times. Nobody is watching your face, only the clever dog.

### Crawling

This is a trick that always fascinates people and can be useful if your dog has to crawl under a fence or stile when out walking. First of all teach it to lie down. Then encourage it to come slowly towards you. If it attempts to get up, command it to go 'down' again. Directly it takes one step towards you praise for all you are worth and reward with food. The Police teach this trick under a net, so the dog has to crawl to get out. It is a very tiring trick so don't make it do it for more than a few steps at first. Many dogs crawl towards you naturally if they are not sure of a welcome. If you can make them do it by looking sad and then show pleasure, this is the easiest way of all, as anything developed naturally always makes the best trick.

### Begging

This is an easy trick to teach. Make the dog sit, while you hold an enticing titbit over its nose. It will reach up to get it. Only give it if the dog stays sitting on its hind legs but lifts its front paws off the floor. Day by day get it to sit up more and more, and then make it wait a second before having the titbit. Soon it will do this trick on its own just to get a titbit. Some people like to add the trick 'trust' to this by placing a piece of sugar on the dog's nose. Hold it there for the first few times with the word 'trust' in a very firm tone, then throw it off the nose with a jerk and say 'paid for' in a light, happy tone of voice and love your dog. This can be a useful trick as you can get friends to offer

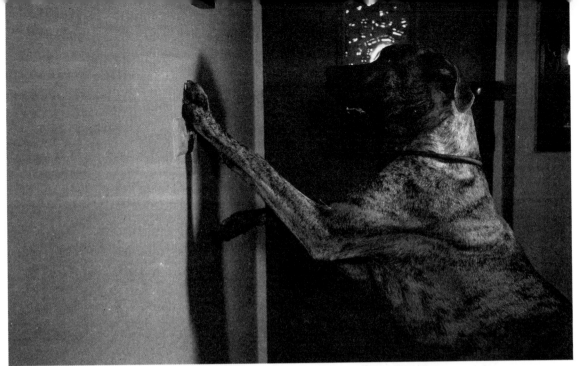

*Juno was able to perform a number of tricks, turning out the light being one of them.*

*titbits and make the dog refuse them by saying 'trust'. Then when you offer the same titbit and say 'paid for' the dog will take it, thereby learning not to take food from strangers. This might save its life if a burglar offered it food.*

### Closing the Door

*Begin by running up with the dog to the door and giving the command 'jump', if necessary lifting the dog's paws up to the door. Reward as usual. Always make it sound exciting to do. Next pat the door and say 'jump' and hold a piece of meat up on the door. The dog will jump up to get the food. Praise him tremendously when he does this. Soon the dog will rush to the door on the command and push it. Big dogs can be taught to close the door by pulling on the handle. This is taught after the dog has learnt to retrieve anything that it is told. On the command 'hold' and being shown the door handle the dog will close its mouth on it. Then give the command 'pull' and help the dog to pull the door gently. If it pulls it even a few inches give the reward and lots of praise. Always tell the dog how very clever it is.*

*'Die for the Queen' is taught by getting a dog to drop into the down position on the command 'down' which slowly changes to 'down die' and then 'die' only. Next the dog is pushed on to its side after it has dropped to the 'down', and the word 'die' repeated as often as possible. It should stay in that position until the words 'Good girl' or some similar remark indicate that the trick is over. I always got my Juno to crawl and then die as one trick; it is useful for film work if the dog is supposed to be injured.*

*Before you can teach a dog any really*

*outstanding household tricks (I don't like circus tricks) it should reach a high standard of obedience in ordinary things. Obedience training develops the dog's brain, and in my opinion true companionship is only found in an obedient dog belonging to a loving owner.*

*Juno knew so many tricks I couldn't think of anything more to teach her. In films she pulled a baby away from a river, and dragged a man out of a room by the arm, without even marking his arm with her teeth, in spite of the fact that she had to growl hard all the time she was doing it, and look terrifyingly fierce. She put a hot-water bottle in a child's bed, played french cricket, carried a poodle puppy and dropped it gently into the dirty linen basket and shut the lid on it, and fetched a bottle of whisky from a cupboard for a tramp. Anything that it is possible for a dog to do she did. I never taught her more than two or three minutes before she was wanted to do something, as I knew she would understand and I didn't want to bore her. But that intelligence had only come with years of patience and love, and her intense desire to please me.*

*If you ever want your dog to act in films or on TV, like Juno did, you must teach her to come, or go away, on signals only. It must go with whatever actor you introduce it to without as much as glancing back at you. The dog must obey its owner's spoken commands at the rate of about one a second from any angle. Next time you see a film with a dog in it note whether the dog is looking at the actor or into the distance at its handler. The dog that is apparently looking at a handler is not one hundred-per-cent trained*

# Pet's Corner

## Hamsters

Hamsters make lovely pets and one of the great advantages is they can, if absolutely necessary, be left with enough food and water for a day if you have to be away for some reason as they store food.

They are extremely clean little animals and if you keep their cage clean (wood shavings are best) they have no smell like mice. Don't use newspapers, but white tissues make an excellent bedding.

You can't keep lots of hamsters in a cage together. They fight to the kill, so you have to have a separate cage for each of them. The only time you can leave them together is when the female is ready for mating. They come in to season about every four days and the only way to tell if she is ready for mating is how she behaves towards the male. If she attacks him take her quickly out of the cage. Many of you will not want to breed as

there is the problem of getting rid of the offspring as they have litters of often more than eight. They carry their babies in their womb for 16 days. Be sure to have the females strictly alone when they are having their babies.

Sometimes when you buy a hamster if it is very young it may soil its cage anywhere, but it is remarkable how quickly they choose a spot for their toilet and stick to it.

They very quickly learn

to know you and will answer like a dog to a name. Be very gentle when first stroking it and don't pick it up until you get to know it which doesn't usually take long. If you have just fed it, your hands still smell of food. Wash them before handling it or it may nip your fingers thinking they are food. Go slowly whatever the temptation in handling your new hamster.

Feeding is easy. You can buy hamster food at any pet shop but green food and roots like carrots are very welcome. When you find a diet that suits your hamster stick to it rather than continuously changing and thus perhaps causing a tummy upset.

It is absolutely vital to have a safe cage with a bedroom for resting purposes and don't interfere with your hamster in the resting section as you may get bitten.

If you get very proficient as a hamster owner you may like to take up breeding as a sideline. The variety of colours possible to produce is extensive. So if you ever intend breeding why not make a cage suitable for this purpose. Remember hamsters can eat through wood in seconds so any wood must be covered by wire netting. It must have a safe water drinking vessel and also its cage must be in a warm draught-free place out of the sun. Before you breed ask a pet shop if they will buy your excess stock or you may be lumbered with far in excess of what you want for your own pleasure.

When they are breeding they need extra protein in their food in the form of fish or meat or a boiled egg. Hamsters take a varied diet. Always clean the feeding bowl out daily. Food is inclined to go bad and upset the hamster. Reduce the food if it leaves some over each day. Don't feed beetroot if you have lightly coloured hamsters or they may turn pink from contact with this. Even carrot can stain white hamsters.

It is very easy to tell the sex of a hamster. The female is rounded near her tail and has seven teats. The male is pointed. Lift the hamster by the scruff of the neck to be able to see what sex it is.

Hamsters don't live very long so it is always a good idea to know that at about $2\frac{1}{2}$ years old your hamster may need replacing. 3 years is about the average life span. Buy a new hamster at about 5-6 weeks. Make sure it is tight-eyed, plump and its coat looks healthy and see that it doesn't attack you when you put a finger on top of its cage or you may get some fingers bitten when trying to handle it.

Your pet shop will always help you with any problems you may encounter.

*Left and above:* Golden Hamsters. These lovely animals make excellent household pets and are very popular with children.

These curious facts about the animal world . . .

*Which animal is known as 'The King of Beasts'?*
The lion. He looks magnificent, although he is
not the most savage of all the big cats.

*'The Ship of the Desert' is a name given to which
animal?* The camel. This may be because it
moves both legs together, on each side of its
body, which produces a curious rocking motion,
rather like a ship.

*Which animal has ears so large it uses them as a
fan?* The African elephant. It keeps its ears in
constant motion during the heat of the day.

*Which is considered the most intelligent of all
the apes?* The chimpanzee, as it learns more
quickly than all the others and so can be taught to
perform in an almost human manner. But it
becomes bad-tempered after 7 or 8 years old.

*One furry animal has a bill like a duck, webbed
feet and lays eggs. What is it called?* The duck-
billed platypus. Found only in Australia and
Tasmania, it tunnels out a home in the banks of a
stream.

Animals come in all shapes and sizes, and here are a few record-holders.

*Which is the slowest-moving animal known?* The sloth. It only stays awake a few hours each day, and rarely makes the effort to reach its top speed of half a mile an hour.

*Which is the fastest land animal?* The cheetah, which can reach a speed of 75 miles per hour over a short distance.

*Which is the tallest animal?* The giraffe, which can be over 19 feet high.

*Which is the largest land animal?* The African Bush Elephant, which can weigh over 6 tons.

*Which is the largest living creature?* The blue whale. The female is larger than the male and can grow to more than 30 metres long.

# Pet's Corner

## Guinea pigs

As children I and my family bred guinea pigs and there was great competition as to who could breed the Abyssinian with the most rosettes in its coat and my sister always won. They are utterly charming pets and scream with excitement when they see their owner coming. I think they are always hoping for food and more food, perhaps that is why they are called 'pigs'. Actually the male is called a boar and the female a sow, although they look nothing like pigs. You can get lots of different colours, we mostly had whites and tortoishells. I had some smooth ones as well. When they are one colour they are termed 'selfs'. When they are two or three colours they are called 'marked'.

They are very friendly with each other and lots can safely live together. They don't exercise themselves like rabbits do if let free on grass—rabbits take great leaps, guinea pigs just run about. If handled gently they become extremely tame and usually pet shops buy them if you don't want the babies yourself or an advertisement in a weekly magazine usually brings customers. The Smooth haired ones are named Bolivian or English, the Peruvian have very long hair and take much more seeing after, so I advise most youngsters to have either of the first two I've mentioned.

You can tell the sex of a guinea pig by holding them

*Left:* Silver Agouti Guinea Pigs, female and day-old young. *Above:* Colour varieties of Guinea Pig.

upside down the genital opening in the female is like a V, the male has a round opening and if pressed very gently the penis can be seen quite plainly.

You house guinea pigs the same way as rabbits—lay some sawdust and ontop plenty of meadow hay—If you keep them outside they need keeping dry and sheltered in winter and out of very strong sun in summer. Many people buy pellets for them these days, but they do need vegetables, they love apples, carrots swedes and all the cabbage family. They love brown bread and milk, oats, bran and they should have added vitamins like a crushed multivite tablet in winter when fresh vegetables aren't so plentiful. The sun will give them the vitamin D they need.

Try and judge the amount of food needed by the amount they clear up each day when you first get them. Never leave stale food either green-stuff or cereal etc; it will soon go bad and could give them diarrhoea. Always leave water in the cage.

You mustn't pick a guinea pig up by its scruff as you can a rabbit, pick them up by the neck and the other 'hand under the hind quarters.

You must soon get your guinea pig to like being brushed. You don't need a hard brush, even a toothbrush can do the job quite well. I used to use a baby's hair brush. Always brush the rosettes the way they grow from the body and the smooth ones must be brushed the way the coat grows.

When breeding, the boar can stay with the females until the babies are about to be born but remove him before the birth as you don't want the sow to be mated too soon again. The babies are born with their eyes open and with hair, quite different from the rabbits. The sow carries her babies for 63 days, it is amazing how soon they become active and eating. We usually wean them at about 5 weeks when the sexes should be segregated as they should not be allowed to have a litter under at least six months.

If your garden is safe the guinea pigs can be allowed out of their cages for exercise provided they are tame enough to catch again otherwise have a roll of wire netting and make a circle of it so at least you can catch them.

See their nails don't get too long if they are always on grass, these should be cut with a guillotine not clippers as they are inclined to pinch If you can't do it yourself you may have to get your Vet to do it, as if the nails turned over the animal would be very uncomfortable, it doesn't often happen with plenty of exercise. Keep a good look out for lice and wash the animal with a medicated soap or ask your Vet for something as lice cause the animal not to thrive.

# Giving A Dogs' Party

HAVE you ever thought of having a dogs' party at Christmas for all your friends? Naturally you have to have a large room or hall for it, but you can raise a lot of money for charity by running one.

It is fun and it shows how well your dog is trained. The dogs love the excitement and join in all the games.

We always start with 'Musical sits', played the same way as musical chairs except that rings chalked on the floor are used instead of chairs, starting of course with one ring less than there are dogs and owners. The music starts and all the dogs walk sedately round the room. When the music stops everyone tries to find a circle and get his dog sitting in it. Some of the not-so-well-trained think this is just their chance to jump up at their owners, which makes it difficult for the owners to run to a ring spot. The dog that fails to find an unoccupied ring is out, and each time the numbers are reduced one circle is rubbed out. The dash for the last remaining ring is always most exciting.

Next comes the thread-the-needle race with dogs on a lead over the owner's right wrist. Owner and dog run up to a partner and the owner then threads the needle with the hand that holds the dog. If you are left handed you will, of course, have the lead on your left hand. If you have never tried threading a needle with a naughty, fidgety dog tied to your wrist, it is an experience that will egg you on to train your dog to sit still when told. To complete the course you must run back to the starting point.

The next game consists of preparing beforehand thirty cut-out pictures of dogs and pasting them on boards, leaving out the breed of the dog. The guests are given ten minutes to try their skill at determining the breed of each.

A 'breather' after an energetic game is to ask the teams to take turns in picking pieces of dog photographs or drawings from boxes marked 'heads', 'bodies', and 'tails'. The team to get six dogs put together correctly wins.

And lastly we have the scent discrimination game in which—for the dog owner—the boot is on the other foot, so to speak. Every guest is asked to bring a little cotton bag containing some sort of distinctive scent, each decided beforehand so as to make them all different, for example, an onion, eau-de-cologne, mint, eucalyptus, etc. Then the owners are blindfolded and led to a table where these scents are spread out in their bags side by side. You would be surprised how hard the guests find it to pick out their own bag.

Extra items like fancy dress, and a prize for the dog that can do most tricks, always add to the fun.

Next we have a team fetch-and-carry race, each unit of the teams consisting of a dog and two people well known to it. Dog and owners of each team line up at one end of the room, while the third member of each unit lines up in the same order at the other, holding a favourite article belonging to the dog he or she is paired with. On the signal to start the first dog is called to the person holding its possession, which it must take back to its owner. As soon as it has delivered it over a certain line owner and dog go to the back of the team and the next dog repeats the action. The first team to have all their articles delivered wins. It is not an easy game, because success depends on the dog's response to the caller, and on his carrying the article safely back.

Kim's game is another that is played with articles that belong to the dogs; dog biscuit, collar, lead, feeding bowl, comb, brush, name tally, nail clippers, ball, blanket, condition powders, etc. The guests look at the collection of these things for one minute and then try and remember what they saw. The guest with most correct articles listed is the winner.

Next we have a large drawing of a tailless dog and the blindfolded guests have to try to fix its tail in the right position. A relay race for owners and dogs is more energetic and there are usually a few spills here, because unless the dogs are well trained they may try to play with the others even though they are on the lead. Owners divide into two teams, each with their dogs on leads, and on the word 'go' each in turn must dash up to the end of the hall, round a human post and back over a line before the next person may start. The first team to finish wins.

THE problem that all dog owners have to find an answer for at some time or other is whether to take their dog with them on holiday, leave him at home with neighbours, or put him in boarding kennels.

I don't have to find an answer myself, because any dog of mine would break her heart if I left her, and I am sure many of my readers' dogs would too. So if a dog I had could not accompany me wherever I went, I would not take a holiday. That means that in the dog's lifetime a holiday abroad is ruled out. It is one of the sacrifices that dog lovers make willingly in return for the love and affection of their dogs.

Let us suppose that you have every intention of taking your dog with you on holiday. What must you do to prepare him for this venture? First of all start training him to lie quietly for long periods when you leave him and go out of sight. That is not taught in a day, and if you neglect this lesson you will indeed have a miserable time in your boarding house or hotel, for in most hotels dogs are allowed only in the bedrooms. If not trained to stay quietly alone, he may bark, tear things up, scratch at the door, or even be sick with anxiety. Teach him step by step to stay, first of all

nobody. Many people don't like dogs and if yours jumps up on everyone, there will be unpleasantness. On the other hand, people often cause you annoyance by not leaving your dog alone, and the poor creature has to put up with endless unwanted caresses. I always tried to explain that my dog was a trained one, and taught to ignore other people, and that by petting her they were putting a big strain on her.

Always see that your dog lies out of the way in some corner; nobody likes having to step over a dog in the passage.

Never allow your dog up on the bed; you may not object, but other people don't like to sleep under bedclothes that dogs have been on, and eiderdowns can't be cleaned between guests' visits.

Always take his favourite blanket, so that when you leave him, he will have something of his own from the very first. If you have an indoor kennel take it with you and put it up in your bedroom.

If you have your dog on the beach with you, make sure he doesn't commit the quite unforgiveable sin of lifting his leg over someone's clothes or deck chair. If you allow him to cause offence you are a disgrace to dog owners.

# Taking Your Dog On Holiday

with you in sight, then get further away each day. He will soon learn that you are coming back and will relax and eventually go to sleep. It is all a matter of giving him confidence in you, then he will trust you to come back to him. You must be very firm if he gets up when told to stay. A weak-willed owner seldom succeeds with this lesson.

Next, if you have a car, teach him to stay quietly in it, for when travelling you may wish to enter a restaurant where dogs aren't allowed. Should your dog howl or bark when you leave him, rush back and sound very angry, pull him firmly to the 'down' position by his choke chain, repeat the command 'down stay' until the dog grasps what he has to do. Then, when he stays quietly for a few seconds at first, love and praise him.

If you are travelling by train, he may have to go into the guard's van, especially if the train is crowded, so accustom him to wearing a light leather muzzle, long before the journey makes this necessary. Few guards insist on this if it is a friendly dog, but they have a right to do so.

When you arrive at your hotel enquire in which rooms your dog is allowed. Be sure to see that he causes annoyance to

Salt water is extremely bad for a dog's skin. If yours likes bathing, see if you can rinse him fairly often in clean warm water, and when going on holiday be sure to take towels for him.

Try to give him at least one big run a day out in the country or on an unfrequented part of the beach, so that there is no risk of his soiling pavements or a frequented beach. Remember that children run about barefoot and sunbathers in scanty suits lie about, and dogs can be unpleasant in their habits.

Make sure that the right food is available for him wherever you go. If you suddenly change his diet he may get a tummy upset, which would be most annoying on holiday. You can always order his favourite food from a local grocer or butcher or pet shop. If this is impossible, get a supply sent on in advance. You don't want to worry about that sort of thing on holiday.

Make sure that your dog is the perfect example of what a trained dog should be, so that if you wish to return to the same place another year you will be welcome and – perhaps more important – you will not have prejudiced the landlady against having anyone else's dog.